I0797959

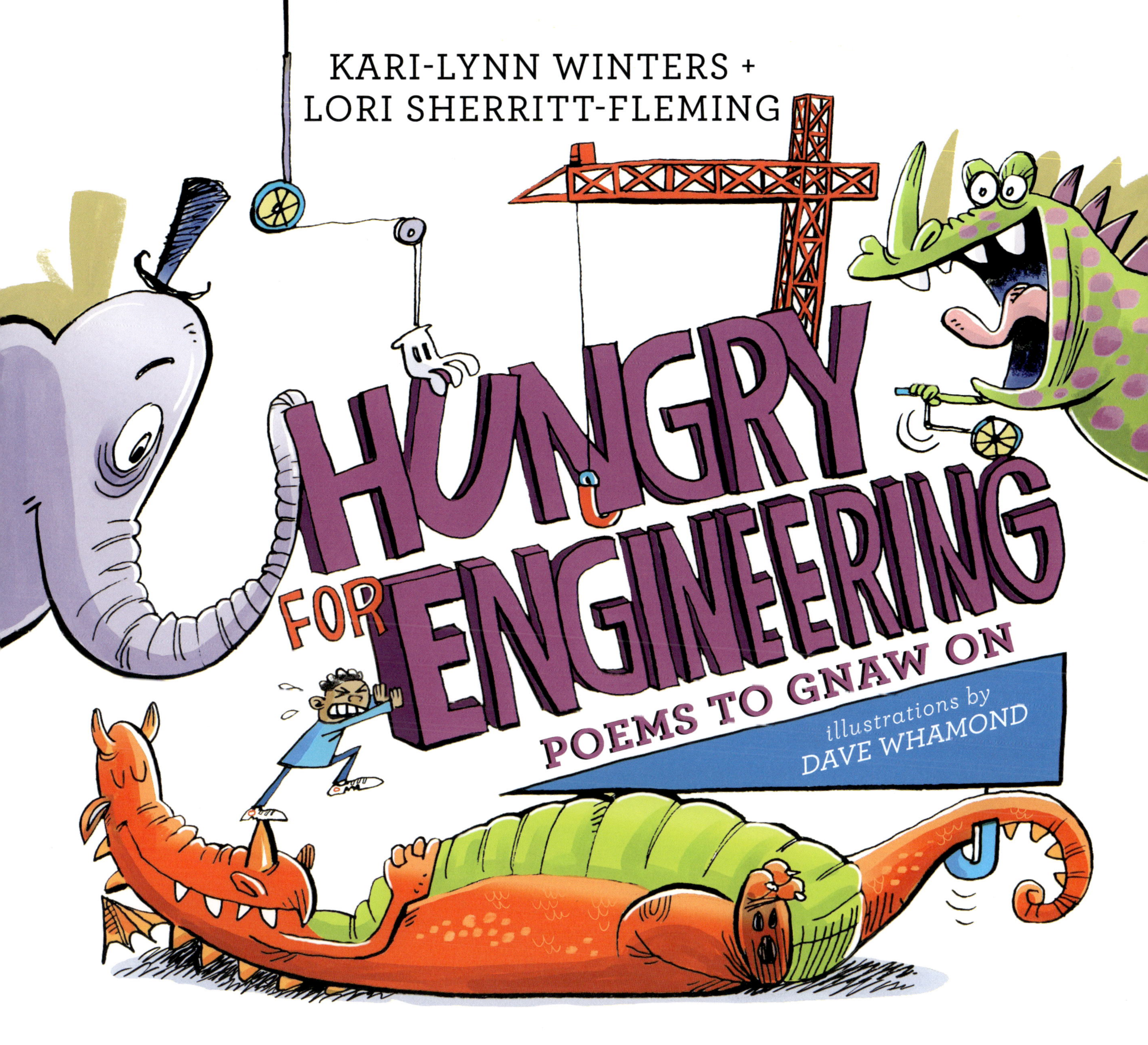
KARI-LYNN WINTERS +
LORI SHERRITT-FLEMING
HUNGRY FOR ENGINEERING
POEMS TO GNAW ON
illustrations by
DAVE WHAMOND

Published in Canada by Fitzhenry & Whiteside,
209 Wicksteed Avenue, Unit 51, Toronto, ON M4G 0B1

Published in the United States by Fitzhenry & Whiteside,
60 Leo Birmingham Pkwy, Suite 107, Brighton, MA 02135

Fitzhenry & Whiteside acknowledges with thanks the Canada Council for the Arts and the Ontario Arts Council for their support of our publishing program. We acknowledge the financial support of the Government of Canada through the Canada Book Fund (CBF) for our publishing activities.

Library and Archives Canada Cataloguing in Publication
Title: Hungry for engineering : poems to gnaw on /
Kari-Lynn Winters + Lori Sherritt-Fleming ;
illustrations by Dave Whamond.
Names: Winters, Kari-Lynn, 1969- author | Sherritt-Fleming, Lori, 1968- author. | Whamond, Dave, illustrator
Description: Includes index.
Identifiers: Canadiana 2024041666X | ISBN 9781554556427 (hardcover)
Subjects: LCGFT: Poetry.
Classification: LCC PS8645.I5745 H84 2024 | DDC jC811/.6—dc23

Publisher Cataloging-in-Publication Data (U.S.)
Names: Winters, Kari-Lynn, 1969- author | Sherritt-Fleming, Lori, 1968- author | Whamond, Dave, illustrator.
Title: Hungry for engineering : poems to gnaw on / Kari-Lynn Winters + Lori Sherritt-Fleming ; illustrated by Dave Whamond.
Description: Toronto, Ontario : Fitzhenry & Whiteside Limited, 2024. | Summary: A collection of poems describes how to use wedges, inclined planes, pulleys, and screws to design, innovate, and construct a luxurious bug hotel, a fun marble run, and a mighty wind tower strong enough to blow you over the ocean" – Provided by publisher.
Identifiers: ISBN 978-1-55455-642-7 (hardcover)
Subjects: LCSH: Engineering – Juvenile poetry. | Simple machines – Juvenile poetry. | Engineering design – Juvenile poetry. | Children's poetry, Canadian. | BISAC: JUVENILE NONFICTION / Poetry / Humorous.
Classification: LCC PR9199.4.W7878 H936 2024 | DDC 811/.54 – dc23

Dave Whamond's original art for this book was drawn traditionally with ink and pen/paper. Colour was added and the artwork was then scanned. Watercolour, chalk, and other media were added through a digital program.

Cover and text design by Tanya Montini
Printed in Canada by Copywell

fitzhenry.ca

To Tiffany, Alison, and Scott, my research colleagues,
for always keeping the TEAM in our project's
STEAM-powered adventures.

•

And to Lori and Jean, and my BAM writing pals,
for keeping the gears turning and
fine-tuning the poetic beats.

—KL

To all of those who dream big, think out of the box and
occasionally find a place for an extra syllable.

—LSF

For my son, Zachary, who is a budding engineer.
With LEGO, but still!

—DW

FILTERED
WATER

HUNGRY FOR ENGINEERING

I crave towers—a tasty treat.
Built with straws and luncheon meat.
A robot sandwich, oh so grand!
With stringy cheese and gears in hand.

I munch on staples, screws, and snaps.
And devour plastic bubble wraps.
I crunch on wood chips, a delightful chew,
dipping them in glittery glue.

I feast on bridges and red rockets,
made from cardboard pizza-pockets!
Filtered water—to wash it down.
Who's the hungriest engineer in town?

CLEAR AS MUD?

I want to be an engineer,
and filter water
to make it clear.

What can I use? Now let me think...
so muddy water is safe to drink...

I choose some cotton and tiny rocks,
and cut some squares from a pair of socks.

Pour brown water through this screen...
Trickling...
s l o w w w w w w w l y.
Will it come out clean?

Should I sip it? No, not right away.
The filtered water still seems grey.

It worked a little, I must admit...
I'll try some more. I will not quit!

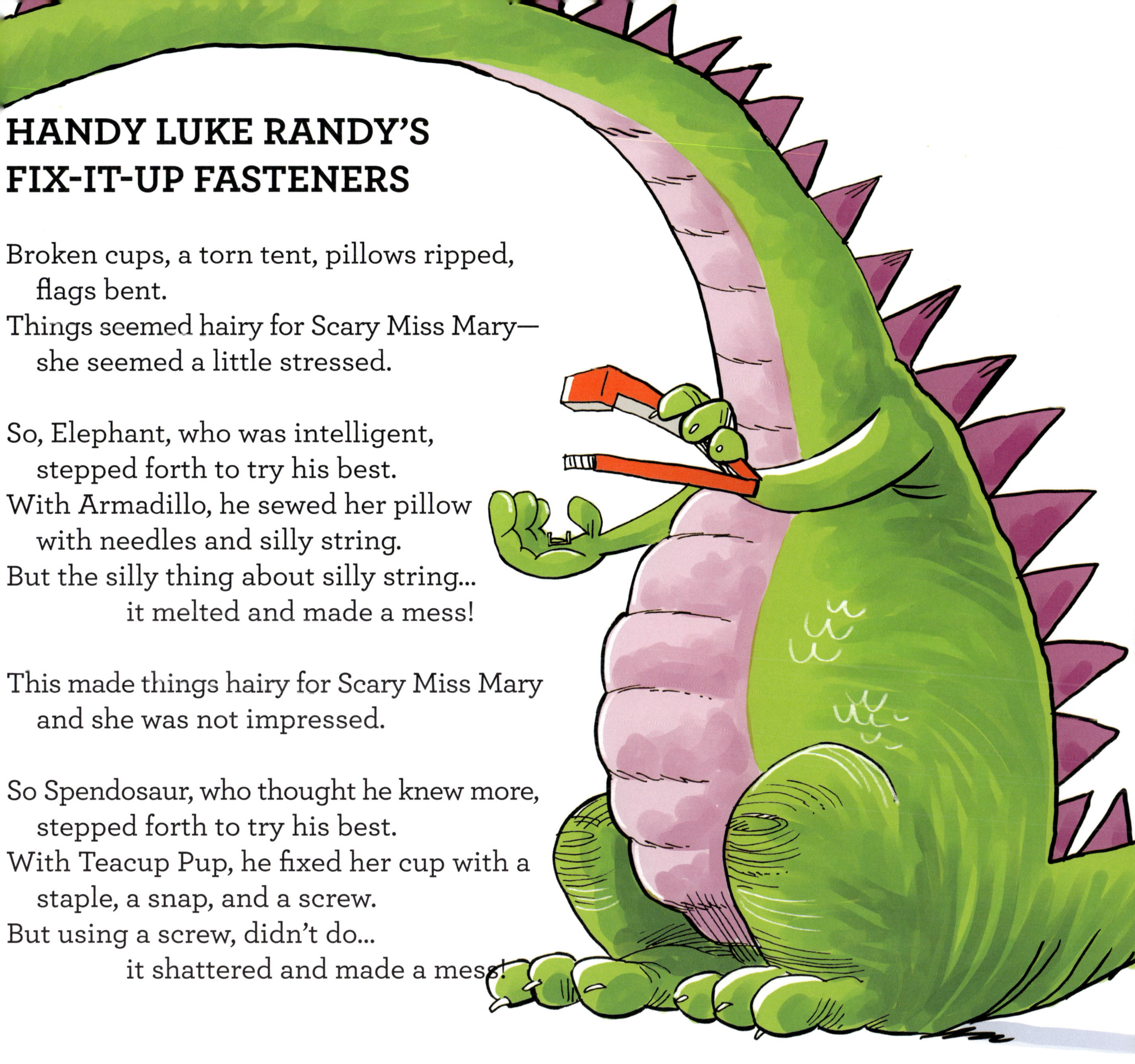

HANDY LUKE RANDY'S FIX-IT-UP FASTENERS

Broken cups, a torn tent, pillows ripped,
flags bent.
Things seemed hairy for Scary Miss Mary—
she seemed a little stressed.

So, Elephant, who was intelligent,
stepped forth to try his best.
With Armadillo, he sewed her pillow
with needles and silly string.
But the silly thing about silly string...
it melted and made a mess!

This made things hairy for Scary Miss Mary
and she was not impressed.

So Spendosaur, who thought he knew more,
stepped forth to try his best.
With Teacup Pup, he fixed her cup with a
staple, a snap, and a screw.
But using a screw, didn't do...
it shattered and made a mess!

BLOOP

This made things hairy for Scary Miss Mary
and she was not impressed.

Now, Luke Randy wasn't so handy, but
stepped forth to try his best.
With Armadillo, he sewed her pillow, with
red and ready thread.
With Teacup Pup, he glued her cup with
blue and ooey goo.
Then, unaware, Luke had to stare...
It worked!
Yes, Ya Hoo!

A bit less hairy for Scary Miss Mary—she
seemed very impressed!

"Excellent!" called Elephant, sounding
loud and a little gruff.
Then, Luke Randy, being handy, fixed the
other stuff.
And Spendosaur knew Luke knew more
(his handiness was the best!),
stated clearly,
and utterly sincerely,
"Now, we shall clean this mess!"

SIMPLE MACHINES.
BUT WHY?

Wedge, wedge, why the edge?
To split two things apart.

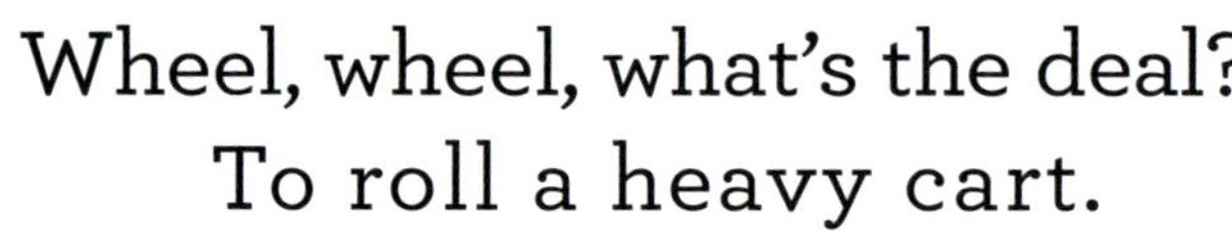

Wheel, wheel, what's the deal?
To roll a heavy cart.

Screw, screw, why choose you?
To fasten things as one.

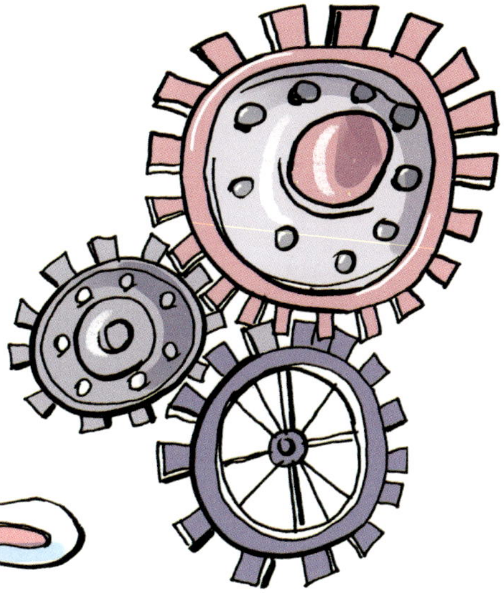

Gear, gear, glad you're here.
To power things to run!

Pulley, ramp, what's your stamp?
To pull and raise things high.

Simple machines!
But why?

To get things done...

Easily

You...

Don't need...

Electricity!

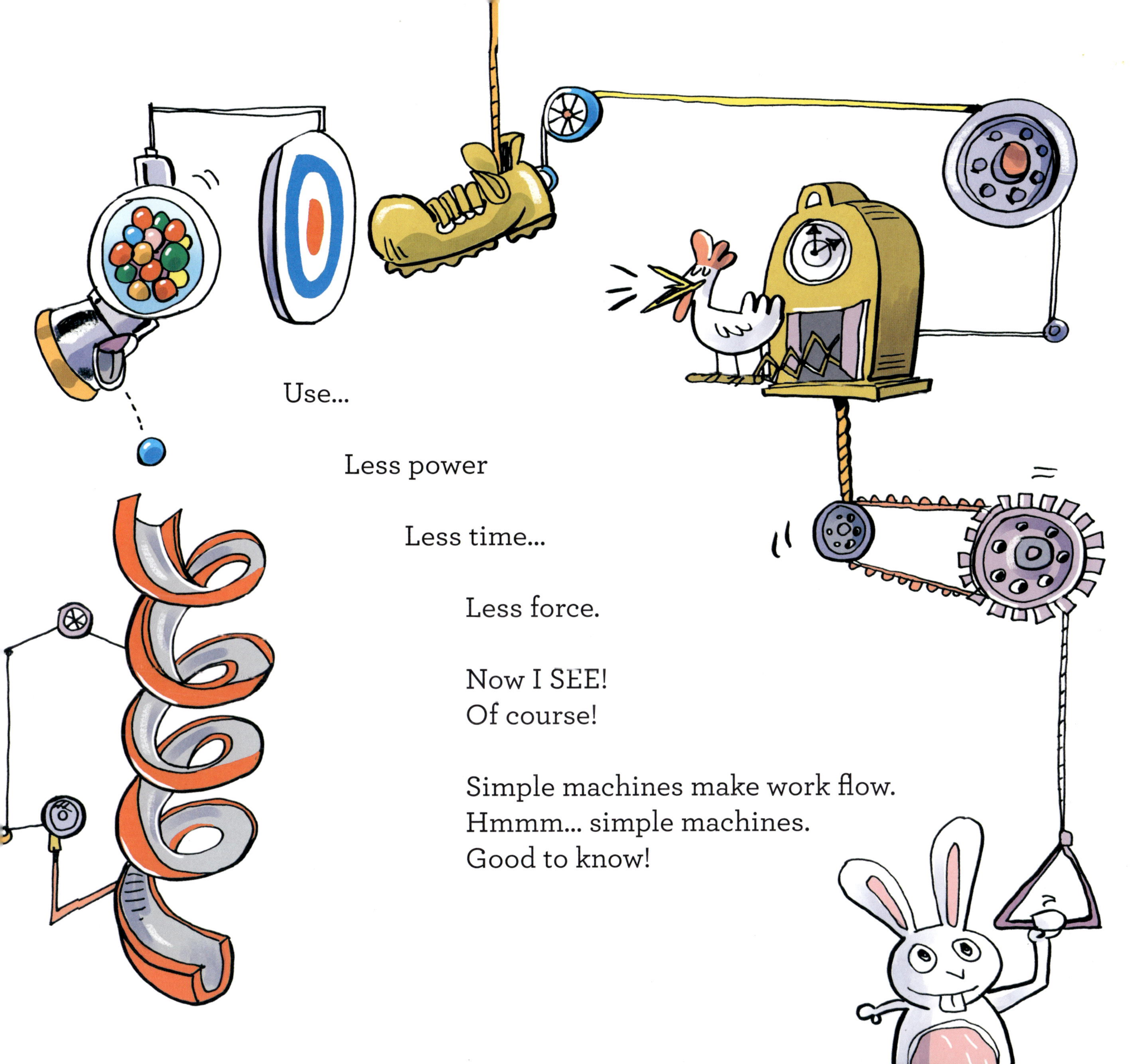

Use...

Less power

Less time...

Less force.

Now I SEE!
Of course!

Simple machines make work flow.
Hmmm... simple machines.
Good to know!

RUN, MARBLE RUN!

First I made my marble GO.
I watched it's speedy D
R
O
P.

When it reached the inclined plane,
I knew it wouldn't STOP.

It twirled around the LOOPTY-LOOP
and then I saw it F
A
L
L,

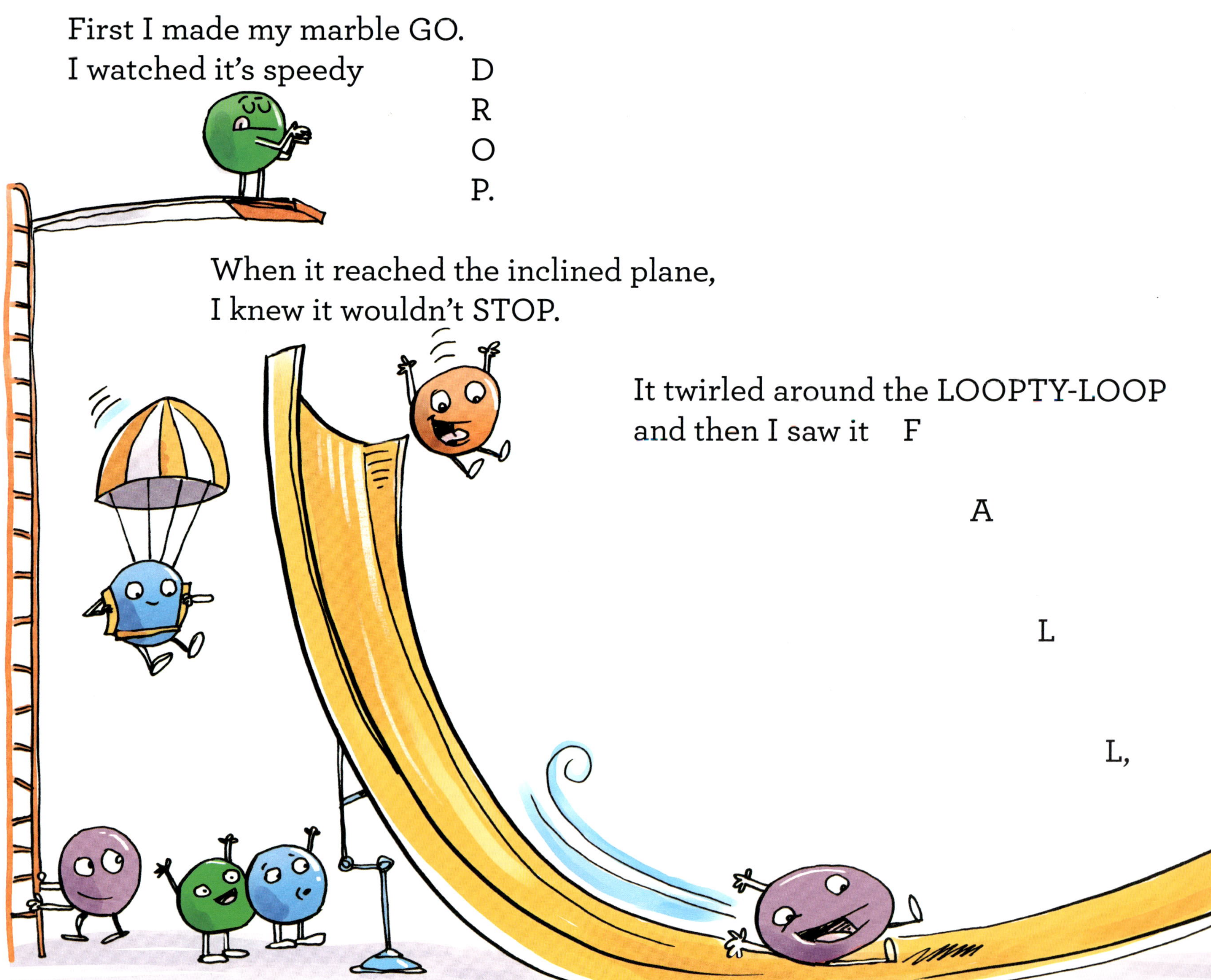

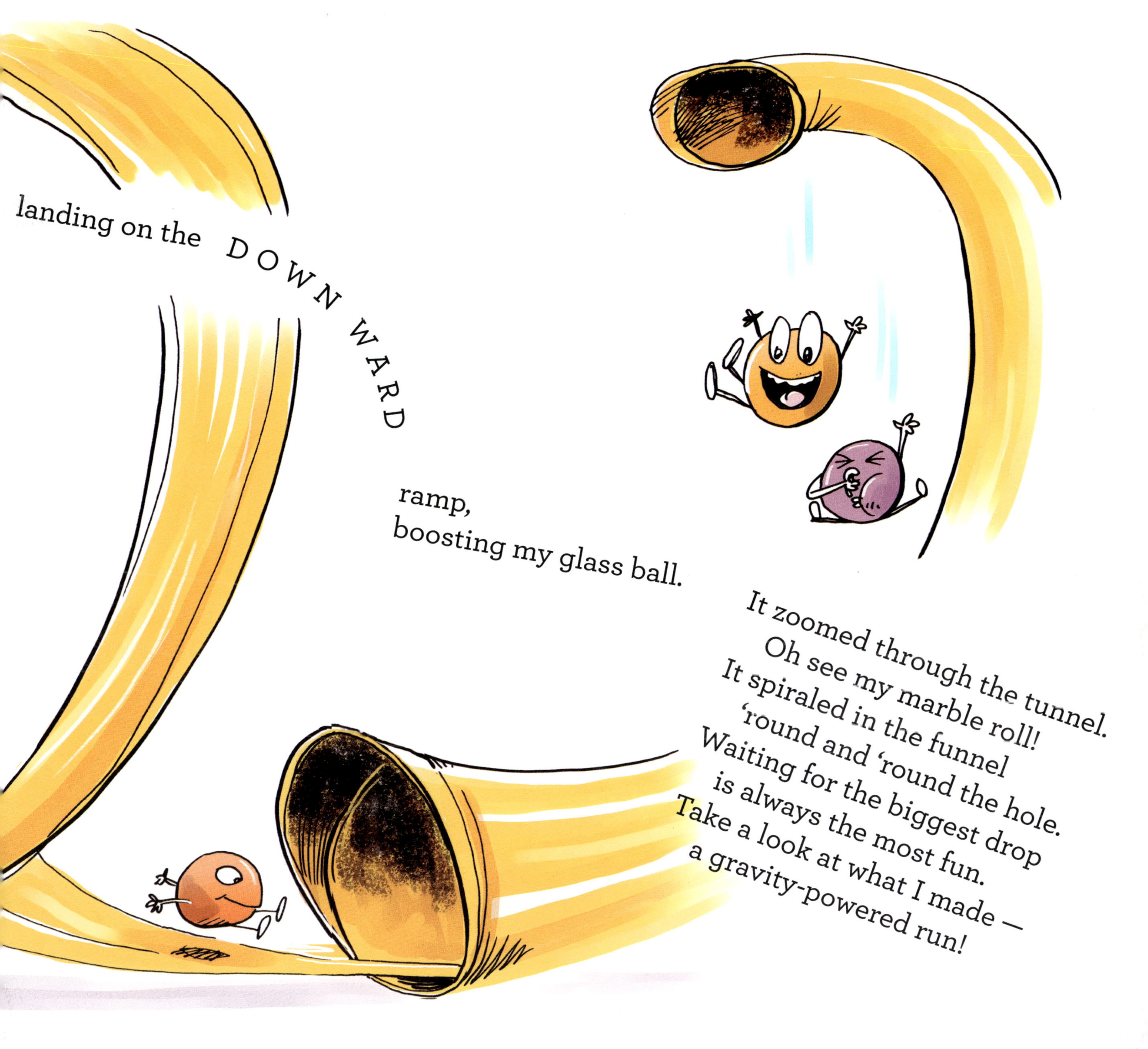

landing on the D O W N W A R D

ramp,
boosting my glass ball.

It zoomed through the tunnel.
Oh see my marble roll!
It spiraled in the funnel
'round and 'round the hole.
Waiting for the biggest drop
is always the most fun.
Take a look at what I made —
a gravity-powered run!

HOW DO YOU WAKE A DRAGON?

How do you wake a dragon, who sleeps in
as a rule?
Till half past eight, each morning, he's
always late for school!

Big sister blares a trumpet,
props the bed with a wedge,
attempts to roll him sideways--
he tumbles off the edge.

Young brother builds a pulley,
and lifts him to his feet,
but his muscles get all achy.
He cries out in defeat.

Dad constructs a lever.
Turns out, it's a flop!
The load's far too heavy.
They all decide to stop.

How do you wake a dragon?
What would ***you*** do?
Would you use a wheel and axle?
An inclined plane? A screw?

How do you wake a dragon who sleeps
in every day?
Try to solve the problem,
I know ***you'll*** find a way!

FLOP!

RUN BY THE SUN

Inventor, Liam O'Leary,
has quite the interesting theory.
He'll capture the sun,
make his toaster run,
then chase it until he is weary.

WIND TOWER POWER

There once lived a girl, Marianne,
Who needed a much bigger fan.
She built a wind tower,
it had so much power,
it blasted her off to Japan!

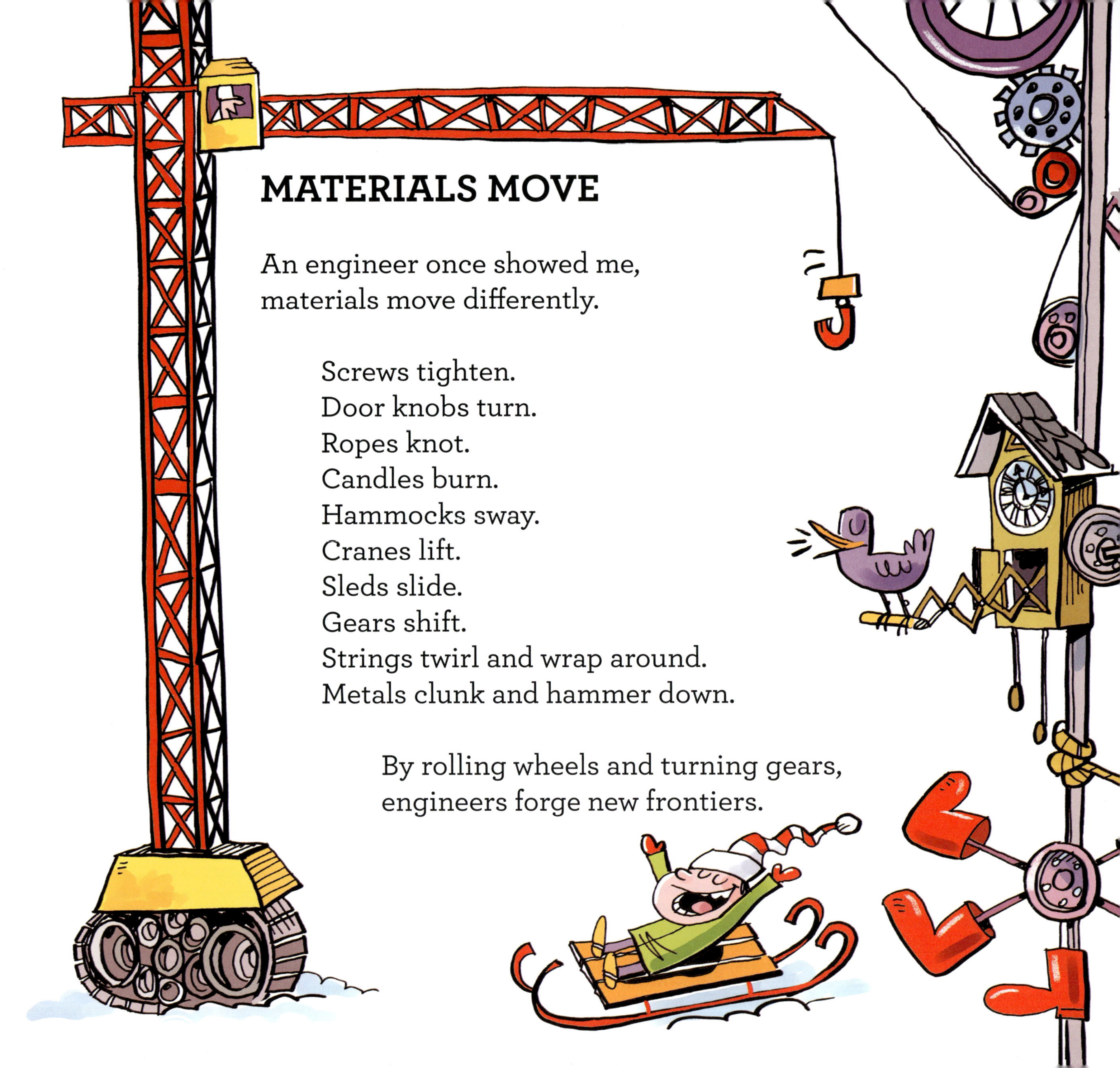

MATERIALS MOVE

An engineer once showed me,
materials move differently.

Screws tighten.
Door knobs turn.
Ropes knot.
Candles burn.
Hammocks sway.
Cranes lift.
Sleds slide.
Gears shift.
Strings twirl and wrap around.
Metals clunk and hammer down.

By rolling wheels and turning gears,
engineers forge new frontiers.

EGG DROP

Egg drop, egg drop number eight,
bubble wrapped like fragile freight,
packed in boxes stuffed with straw,
will it land without a flaw?

Yes...no...maybe...
OHHHHHH!!!

Egg drop, egg drop number nine,
with your parachute so fine,
will it work, or will its fate,
be to smash like number eight?

Yes...no...maybe...
OHHHHHH!!!

Egg drop, egg drop, number ten,
engineered by Jess and Jenn,
with its structure built around,
will it land all safe and sound?

Yes...no...maybe...
OHHHHHH!!!

Hey! It worked!
What's their trick?
Their egg fell, just like a brick.

But...
when it landed—it's a fact,
it stayed whole, remained intact!

BEGONIA'S BUG HOTEL

Begonia built a bug hotel,
turns out she was quite wise.
Her simple backyard project
became an enterprise.

With twigs and leaves and cardboard,
pine cones and paper rolls,
woodchips, bricks and bits of bark,
and logs with drilled-in holes...

Begonia's place was welcoming
for ladybugs and bees.
But not so much for aphids,
who eat every plant they please.

It was *'beneficial'* insects
she wanted to attract,
And lucky her, within a day,
every room was packed!

If you're an eco-friendly bug,
who's into conservation,
call Begonia any time
to make your reservation.

Aphids: Tiny bugs that cause damage to crops. Most species of aphids are not considered to be beneficial insects.

Beneficial Insects: Insects that do helpful gardening and farming jobs such as pollinating and controlling pests. Some examples are: ladybugs, bees, wasps, dragonflies and ground beetles.

Engineering: How people–using math, science, and creativity–invent, design, and build things and solve problems.

Fasteners: Devices such as buttons, zippers, screws, or small hooks that hold things together.

Filters: Fine strainers or nets that clean and separate materials.

Gears: These wheels with teeth or cogs fit together and allow machines to turn faster and operate with more power.

Inclined Planes: Slanted surfaces or ramps that make it easier to move heavy loads to higher or lower ground.

Levers: These simple machines look like see-saws and help raise things up.

Pulley: A wheel and a rope that are used together to help lift heavy items.

Renewable Energy: Power (an energy source) from nature, such as the sun, wind, or water, that never runs out and is good for the earth.

Simple Machines: Devices that make work easier, like gears, levers, pulleys, ramps, screws, wedges, and wheels and axles.

Wedges: Tools with a pointed or sharp edge that help split things apart.